WEALTH

My
VISION BOARD

Financial Freedom
NEXT EXIT

HEALTH

GOOD ♥ HEALTH

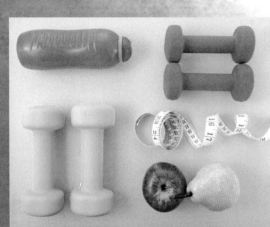

Better Health AHEAD

SELF CARE

FITNESS

TRAVEL

RELATIONSHIPS

Problem solving Skills...

Inspiration
Vision
Knowledge
Idea
CREATIVITY
Motivation
Brainstorm
Innovation
Imagination
Mind

I was created to create

NEW IDEA!

IMPROVE YOUR EFFICIENCY

Focus on Creating Value.

PASSION

Create

MORE FAMILY TIME

FAMILY

peace of mind

WELCOME

GOALS

THIS WEEK

Shine AND SPARKLE!

Be positive

we

need

to

talk

B₃ E₁ L₁ I₁ E₁ V₄ E₁

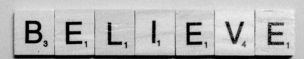

choice

TRAVEL

EMOTIONS

PUFF
LOVE

FRIENDS

CAREER

My Family

Self-reflection check-list

What I am thankful for today?

1.

2.

3.

DEAR SELF, STAY STRONG

feeling BLESSED

TRAVEL

gratitude
CHANGES
every
thing

LEVEL UP

PURPOSE

ACHIEVE YOUR DREAMS

BE pro active

WOW!

conclusion

too
COOL

Smiles
ARE ALWAYS
IN FASHION

DO
MORE
OF
WHAT
MAKES
YOU
HAPPY.

IM **POSSIBLE**

I can & I will

thank you

NO EXCUSES

Small Steps Everyday

INSPIRE   MOTIVATE   IMPROVE

YOU

BE   FOCUS   BE
POSITIVE   CREATIVE

Financial Basics

Seminar

ACHIEVEMENT

YOU MATTER

BALANCE

Stay Honest With Yourself

right for what is thou
relation or from any
point of view.

Confidence

trusting relati nsh
stability, or ve cit
or certainty of a r
for what is

I CAN'T

over Fear

never stop trying

SUCCESS

FEELING LUCKY

BE UNIQUE

BUDGET FOR SUCCESS

RESULTS

VISION

$

Find your purpose!

enjoy

Goal Setting
S	specific
M	measurable
A	attainable
R	relevant
T	time - bound

FAMILY

HARD
WORK
PAYS
OFF

I AM
LIVING MY
DREAM

MEETING

VISION

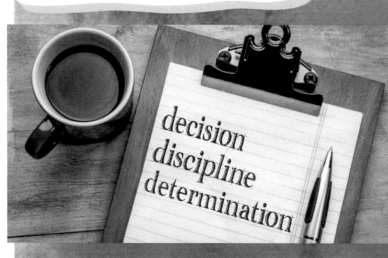

decision
discipline
determination

YES

WHAT'S
NEXT?

PRIORITY

Pessimist

Optimist

NEVER GIVE UP

WHAT'S NEXT?

feeling ALL THE FEELS

I feel _____ because _____

_____

_____

_____

#challenge

future

resolutions deadlines hopes

vision expectations

time ideas goals

plans

LOVE

BE BRAVE

CAREER

CHECK LIST

Today I'm proud that I

-
-
-
-

Tomorrow, I hope...

HOBBY

GOOD
Day

SILENT
SILENT
SPEAK UP
SILENT
SILENT

HABITS

FEAR

COURAGE

pointe
Courage [´k
enables one

MY GOALS

follow
YOUR
heart

Thank you

for choosing our
Vision Board
Clip Art Book

As a special GIFT
I am offering you a
complimentary guide to
download.

This guide is designed to help
you confidently create your
vision board, set SMART
goals, and embrace unlimited
possibilities for your dreams.

Open the camera on your phone
(as if you're going to take a photo)
Hold the phone on the QR CODE below then
a link will appear on your screen
Tap on the link to get your FREE GUIDE

FREE GUIDE

Your Guide to
Creating the Life You
Dream Of

*designed to help you clarify your values, align your beliefs, and set
actionable, meaningful goals that reflect your true self*

Leen W. Hart

Much Love
Leen

Made in United States
Orlando, FL
30 December 2024

56705305R00029